To Michael & Caleb —
Follow your dreams and live a life of love & happiness!
♡ Cheri Jones

DEDICATION

To my husband Kent, for always supporting me while I chase my dreams.

To my illustrator and mentor Bob Fuller, for making it all possible.

— *Cheri Jones*

The scanning, uploading and distribution of this book via the internet or any other means without the permission of the publisher is illegal and punishable by law. Please purchase only authorized electronic editions, and do not participate in or encourage electronic piracy of copyrighted materials. Your support of the author's rights is appreciated.

ISBN: 978-1-7345414-0-3

Copyright ©2019 by Cheri Jones. All rights reserved.
Published by Cheri Jones Publishing Inc.

Visit us online: www.jemainethegoat.com

First Edition
Printed in China.

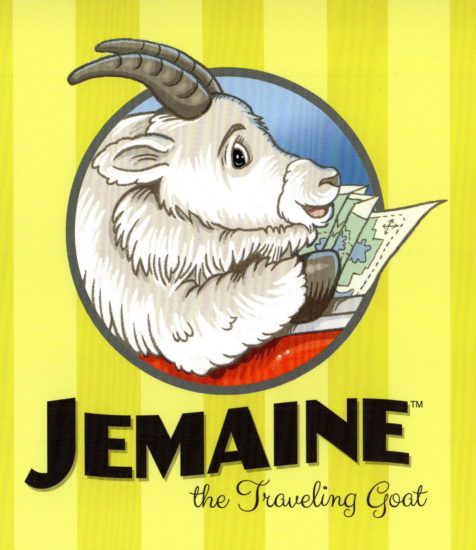

Jemaine™
the Traveling Goat

Written by Cheri Jones

Illustrations by Bob Fuller

I had been sitting on the shelf for weeks, dreaming about my forever family. When would they walk through the door, notice just how special I am and take me away?

Don't get me wrong, I like the Visitor Center, but it does get a little lonely around here.

The Logan Park Visitor Center is the highest point you can drive to on the Going-to-the-Sun Road in Glacier National Park in the wonderful state of Montana. The road can be dangerous, with tight turns, steep cliffs and breathtaking views – It's the perfect place for a young "kid" like me.

You see, I'm a mountain goat, born at the top of the world in the Rocky Mountains. That means I am brave and adventurous, not to mention charming and handsome. Wait — someone is looking my way.

"Oh look honey, isn't that the cutest mountain goat ever? It's just like the real ones we just saw on our hike. Do you think the kids will like him?" asked Mrs. Jones to her husband. "Does it really matter – I think you've already fallen in love," joked Mr. Jones. "But yes, I think the kids will love him too – he's quite handsome."

It sounded like these two had good taste in mountain goats, but would they be the right family for this mountain goat? They mentioned something about "kids." I wonder if they already have mountain goats? I gave them my best sad eyes look... It worked! We headed outside to meet Maddie and Jake.

Maddie rushed to her mother right away and hugged me tight. Jake cried "I want to hold him too!" "Hold on, let's make sure your hands are clean" said Mrs. Jones as she wiped Jake's hands. "We want to keep his fur nice and white."

So far, so good, though I was disappointed that I did not see any other baby mountain goats nearby. And then Maddie asked "What do you think we should name him?" "I know - Snowball, because he looks like snow" replied Jake. "I've got an idea, how about Jemaine, after your Grandpa? He has white hair, people call Grandpa an 'old goat' and I think he would get a kick out of it. Plus, then it's like we are taking Grandpa on our trip with us" suggested Mr. Jones.

With nods and 'Yeahs' all around, I was now 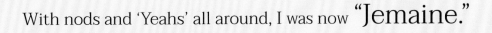"Jemaine."

I was not thrilled – what kind of a name is that? I was going to have to meet this "Grandpa" and decide for myself if he was special enough. But I did not have much time to dwell on it as Mrs. Jones said "All right then kids, everyone in the car. We have a lot more exploring to do before we go back to Many Glacier Hotel for dinner."

That is when I figured it out – human children are also called 'kids'. I was sad that I was not going to be living with any other baby mountain goats. Though they appeared to be a friendly enough bunch, the funny name and lack of other mountain goats were disappointing.

Back in the car, Maddie and Jake took turns holding me as we drove through the rest of the park. Many times we would stop and do a short hike to a clear lake or waterfall. With over 700 miles of trails, we could have hiked all day. Every time we stopped, Maddie would load me into her backpack, so I was able to see everything too.

Well, almost everything...

"Look Jemaine, what a pretty butterfly," Maddie remarked. "I'm afraid he didn't see it facing backwards," said Mr. Jones. "Why don't you wear your backpack on your front side and then his head can peek forward?" "Oh yeah." blushed Maddie. From then on, I had a birds-eye view of the action, plus I was starting to get a little sick traveling backwards!

I knew that my current home was totally awesome, but even I was impressed by the sheer mountain faces, lush greenery and wildflowers. The air was filled with fragrant smells.

"Here's some interesting facts about Glacier National Park – it's huge, larger than the whole state of Rhode Island. There are 130 lakes, and hundreds of different plants and animals. It's the twelfth largest National Park in the US, and a hiker's paradise" Mrs Jones explained.

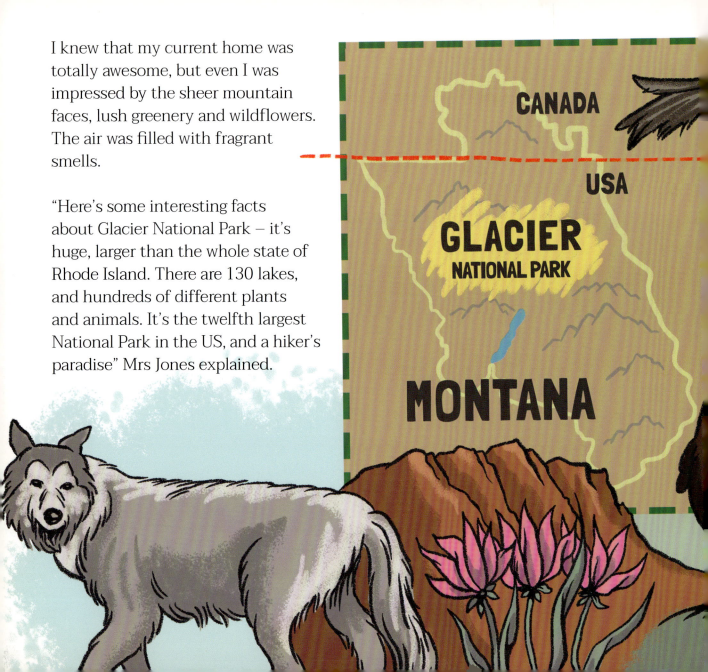

"There are bears, golden eagles and wolves, not to mention bighorn sheep and mountain goats like Jemaine" she continued. Wow, what a great place to be born. I was very proud.

When we finally arrived back at the hotel, everyone was starving. Luckily, Mrs. Jones agreed that I could come along to dinner, and we joined all the other hungry families. "Ugh, I'm stuffed. What's for dessert?" asked Jake. After dinner, we walked outside to watch the sunset. I was surprised to see that we were near a large lake, with mountains stretching high into the sky.

I heard Mr. Jones say that it looked just like a postcard, whatever that means. "I'm bummed that we have to leave tomorrow," Maddie frowned. "Me too," sighed Jake. "It's been fun, but we need to get a good night's rest. We'll be leaving bright and early in the morning for our 16 hour drive home," said Mr. Jones.

That's when it hit me – this wouldn't be my home any more. Where would my new home be? I had no idea how far away a "16 hour drive" would take me. Would I have my lovely mountains and lakes?

I couldn't sleep, worrying about my future, but that did not stop Mr. Jones' excitement the next morning, "It's a long drive, but there's a lot to see along the way. That's the great part about taking a road trip, part of the fun is the adventure!" he said.

After an early breakfast, we were on the road. Boy, was Mr. Jones right, I got to see so much I had never seen before. Large open plains, with snow topped mountains in the distance – it made me wonder even more about my new home.

To pass the time, everyone played car games. "I spy with my little eye... something green," said Mr. Jones. "Those bushes!" Jake shouted. "I know, the grass," said Maddie. "That sign we just passed that said Casper, 100 miles," joked Mom.

Sometimes Maddie and Jake would watch a movie, read a book, or play a video game. I liked just looking out the windows.

It took a long time, but we finally crossed the border into Wyoming. It wasn't much different than Montana, except it was very dry and windy. I must have dozed off, because before I knew it, we were stopping in a city called Cheyenne for dinner.

Shortly after that, Mrs. Jones hit the horn "Honk! Honk!" as we crossed the border into Colorado. Soon Maddie and Jake fell asleep, but I was too excited. I knew we were getting close to my new home.

Late that night, the car stopped and I realized this was it. I wanted to look at everything, but Maddie was exhausted by the long trip and soon I too was asleep in her arms.

The next morning at breakfast, everyone was talking about the trip and how much fun they had. "So kids, what sounds good for a road trip for next year? Maybe Mount Rushmore, the Grand Canyon..." asked Mrs. Jones. "Can we can take Jemaine along with us?" asked Maddie as she hugged me tight. "Yeah," Jake piped in. "Well of course - Jemaine is a member of the family now," said Mrs. Jones.

At that very moment, I knew that wherever home was and whatever lay ahead, this was the right family for me.

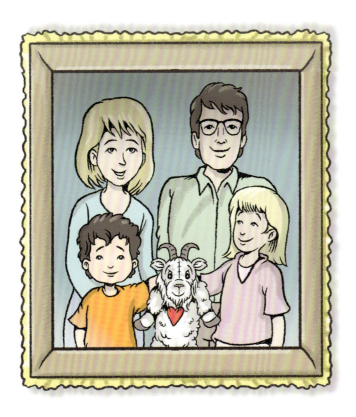

And I could not wait for my **next adventure!**

INTERESTING FACTS ABOUT
MOUNTAIN GOATS

Males are called Billy Goats, Females are called Nanny Goats. Adults weigh between 99 and 309 lbs.

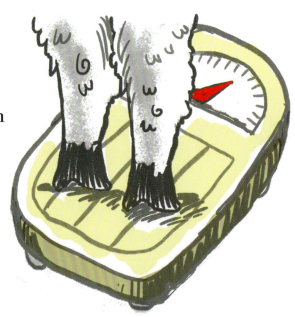

Mountain goats usually live 12-15 years, and stay with thier mother for the first year of life.

They live in the mountains of northwestern North America. (Alaska/Canada/US)

Mountain goats like to eat grasses, moss, herbs and twigs.

Enemies:
- Cougars
- Bears
- Wolves
- Golden Eagles

INTERESTING FACTS ABOUT
GLACIER NATIONAL PARK

Glacier is known as "The Crown of the Continent" due to its beauty and plant and animal life.

There are 61 National Parks in the US, and Glacier is the 8th oldest, founded in 1910.

There are Glaciers in Glacier National Park! There were over 150 active glaciers at one time, but only about 25 today.

The Mountain Goat is the official Park symbol.

Nearly 3 million people visit Glacier each year, making it the 10th most popular National park.

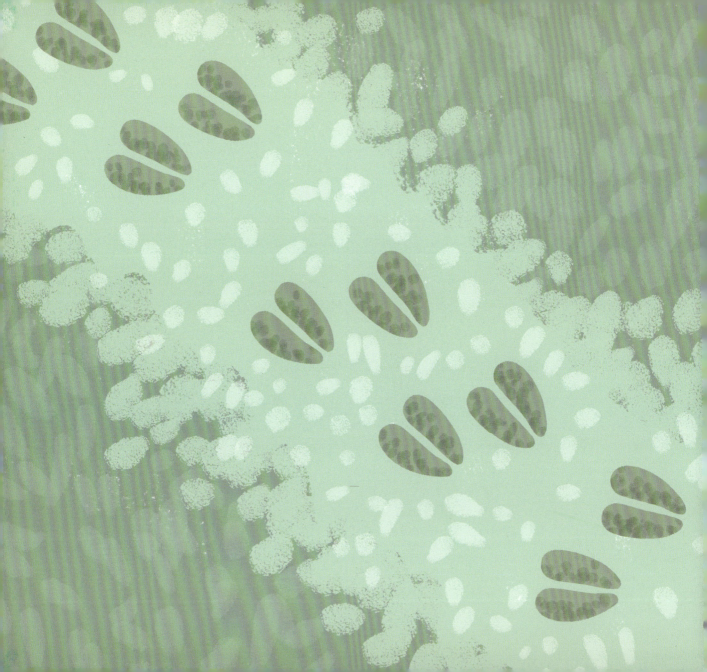